Teaching About
Thanksgiving
With Favorite Picture Books

BY IMMACULA A. RHODES

D1572736

NEW YORK • TORONTO • LONDON • AUCKLAND • SYDNEY
MEXICO CITY • NEW DELHI • HONG KONG • BUENOS AIRES

SCHOLASTIC
Teaching
Resources

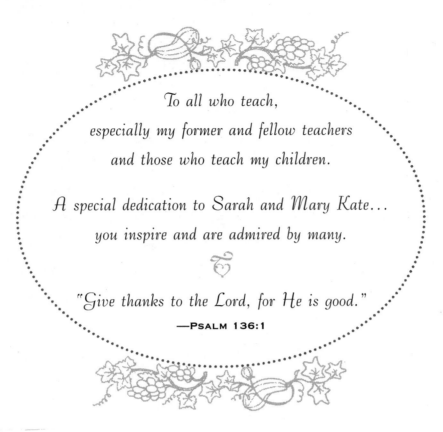

To all who teach,
especially my former and fellow teachers
and those who teach my children.

A special dedication to Sarah and Mary Kate...
you inspire and are admired by many.

"Give thanks to the Lord, for He is good."
—PSALM 136:1

Cover from GRACIAS, THE THANKSGIVING TURKEY by Joy Cowley, illustrated by Joe Cepeda. Illustration copyright © 1996 by Joe Cepeda. Reprinted by permission of Scholastic Inc.

Cover from ON THE MAYFLOWER: VOYAGE OF THE SHIP'S APPRENTICE AND A PASSENGER GIRL by Kate Waters, photographs by Russ Kendall. Photographs copyright © 1996 by Russ Kendall. Reprinted by permission of Scholastic Inc.

Cover from A PLUMP AND PERKY TURKEY by Teresa Bateman, illustrated by Jeff Shelly. Illustrations copyright © 2001 by Jeff Shelly. Reprinted by permission of Winslow House International, Inc.

Cover from SQUANTO'S JOURNEY by Joseph Bruchac, illustrated by Greg Shedd. Used by permission of Harcourt Inc. All rights reserved.

Front cover and interior design by Kathy Massaro
Interior illustrations by Maxie Chambliss

ISBN: 0-439-51785-0
Copyright © 2003 by Immacula A. Rhodes.
Published by Scholastic Inc.
All rights reserved.
Printed in the U.S.A.

3 4 5 6 7 8 9 10   40   09 08 07 06 05

Contents

About This Book

This book offers an array of activities created to help you and your students explore the origin and history of the national U.S. holiday Thanksgiving. In addition to fresh, creative ideas that relate to fact-based, fictional, and humorous Thanksgiving books, you'll find activities that extend beyond each story to incorporate interesting facts and information about the *Mayflower*, the Pilgrims, the Wampanoag people, colonial life, and even turkeys.

Each book unit in *Teaching About Thanksgiving With Favorite Picture Books* includes a wide range of activities and projects designed to enrich students' learning across the curriculum. Resources for further research are also provided to help supplement and extend concepts introduced in the books. And, if you want ideas for including "authentic" Thanksgiving activities in your class celebration, see page 63.

As you and your students explore the books and suggested resources, you'll enrich—and, in some cases, correct—your ideas and knowledge about Thanksgiving. Gather your students and a stack of favorite Thanksgiving books. Then begin an educational journey into the incredible history and traditions of a well-loved holiday.

Getting Started

- ◎ Gather and read the books you plan to use during your Thanksgiving studies. Obtain multiple copies if possible.
- ◎ Prepare a fall table display on which to feature your Thanksgiving books. Arrange other classroom areas to display book- and holiday-related projects.
- ◎ Use the following resources to become familiar with interesting facts and information about Thanksgiving, the *Mayflower*, the Pilgrims, and the Wampanoag people.

Books

Don't Know Much About the Pilgrims by Kenneth C. Davis (HarperCollins, 2002)

Eating the Plates: A Pilgrim Book of Food and Manners by Lucille Recht Penner (Macmillan, 1992)

Wampanoag: People of the East (Plimoth Plantation Educational Materials)

1621: A New Look at Thanksgiving by Catherine O'Neill Grace and Margaret M. Bruchac with Plimoth Plantation (National Geographic Society, 2001)

Web Sites

◎ **Plimoth Plantation**
www.plimoth.org

◎ **The First Thanksgiving: Plimoth,
1621 and Voyage on the Mayflower**
http://teacher.scholastic.com/thanksgiving/
plimoth

http://teacher.scholastic.com/
thanksgiving/mayflower

◎ **Caleb Johnson's MayflowerHistory.com**
http://www.mayflowerhistory.com

◎ **Kid Info Reference Resources:
The Plymouth Colony**
www.kidinfo.com/American_History/
Colonization_Plymouth.html

◎ **The Boston Children's Museum**
www.bostonkids.org/teachers/TC

Connections to the Language Arts and Social Studies Standards

The activities in this book are designed to support you in meeting the following standards outlined by Mid-continent Research for Education and Learning (McREL), an organization that collects and synthesizes national and state K–12 curriculum standards.

Language Arts

Uses the general skills and strategies of the reading process and reading skills and strategies to understand and interpret a variety of literary texts:

◆ Uses meaning clues to aid comprehension and make predictions about content.

◆ Uses reading skills and strategies to understand a variety of familiar literary passages and texts, including fiction and nonfiction.

◆ Knows main ideas or theme, setting, main characters, main events, sequence, and problems in stories.

◆ Makes simple inferences regarding the order of events and possible outcomes.

◆ Relates stories to personal experience.

Uses the general skills and strategies of the writing process:

◆ Uses writing and other methods to describe familiar persons, places, objects, or experiences.

◆ Writes in a variety of forms or genres, including responses to literature.

Social Studies

◆ Understands family life in a community now and in the past (e.g., roles, jobs, cultural traditions, styles of homes).

◆ Understands the history of a local community and how communities in North America varied long ago.

◆ Understands the daily life and values of early Native American cultures.

◆ Understands the reasons that Americans celebrate certain national holidays.

◆ Understands the causes and nature of movements of large groups of people into and within the United States, now and long ago.

Source—(*Content Knowledge: A Compendium of Standards and Benchmarks for K–12 Education* (3rd ed.). (Mid-continent Research for Education and Learning, 2000)

Teaching Activities for Any Time

 nhance, extend, and enlighten students' learning experiences with these activity ideas that connect to language arts and work well with any Thanksgiving-related picture books.

★ Story Timelines ★

 ave children create a timeline of a story's events. Ask them to retell the story, using the timeline as a guide. As a variation, have them draw a story timeline of emotions for a chosen character. Use the timelines to discuss characters' feelings about different events and experiences in the story.

Act It Out!

Invite children to create simple props and costumes and then act out a story (or scene from a story) in mini-play fashion. Or have them make and use puppets to act out their favorite Thanksgiving stories.

Pen Pals

Ask students to name some of the story characters (fictional or real) they would like to know. Then have students write letters to those characters, expressing their desire to meet them. Encourage them to include information about themselves in the letters. Afterward, invite children to read their pen-pal letters to the class. If desired, pretend to be the addressed character and verbally respond to the letter.

Story Element Plates

Help students create story element charts to show the story's characters, plot, setting, problem, and solution. For fun, write each of the elements for several stories on separate six-inch paper plates. Make sure the stories have different characters and vary enough so that no two story elements are identical (for example, each story should have a different setting). Then give each child a plate. On a signal, have children group themselves to bring all the elements in one story together. Then have each group retell its story. (TIP: For self-checking purposes, you might affix identical mini-stickers to the back of each plate belonging to the same story.)

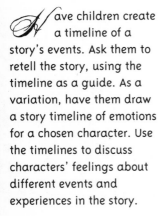

Personal Perspectives

Ask children to write firsthand descriptions of the story characters and their experiences. Then have students sign their character names on their papers. Put the descriptions in a paper bag. During group time, pull out and read one paper at a time. Challenge children to guess the identity of each character.

I wanted the whole country to celebrate Thanksgiving together. I wrote articles and letters about it. Most of the presidents didn't like my idea, but Abraham Lincoln said, "yes" to it. He made Thanksgiving a holiday.

Sarah Hale

I answered a "Turkey Wanted" sign. I got a job as a model for an art show. At the end I left really fast and took an oatmeal turkey with me. I saw the people on Thanksgiving Day. They didn't have turkey because I got away.

Pete

Make Bookmarks

Have children create bookmarks for their favorite stories. Ask them to illustrate and write (or dictate) a summary of the story on the bookmarks. If desired, students can draw and cut out a book character, then glue it to the top of their bookmarks.

Fact, Fiction... or Both?

After reading each story, have children write its title under one of these chart headings: "Fact," "Fiction," or "Fact-based Fiction." For the books listed under "Fact-Based Fiction," ask children to create a chart to sort the factual information from the fictional.

Alphabet of Thanksgiving

Set up an alphabet display to add to throughout your Thanksgiving unit. To prepare, color and cut out 26 turkeys (page 8). Glue each turkey to a separate sheet of large construction paper in a fall color. Label each turkey with a letter, then display all the turkeys in alphabetical order. After reading each story, have children brainstorm things related to Thanksgiving. Ask volunteers to write their responses on the turkey page that corresponds to the first letter of their response.

7

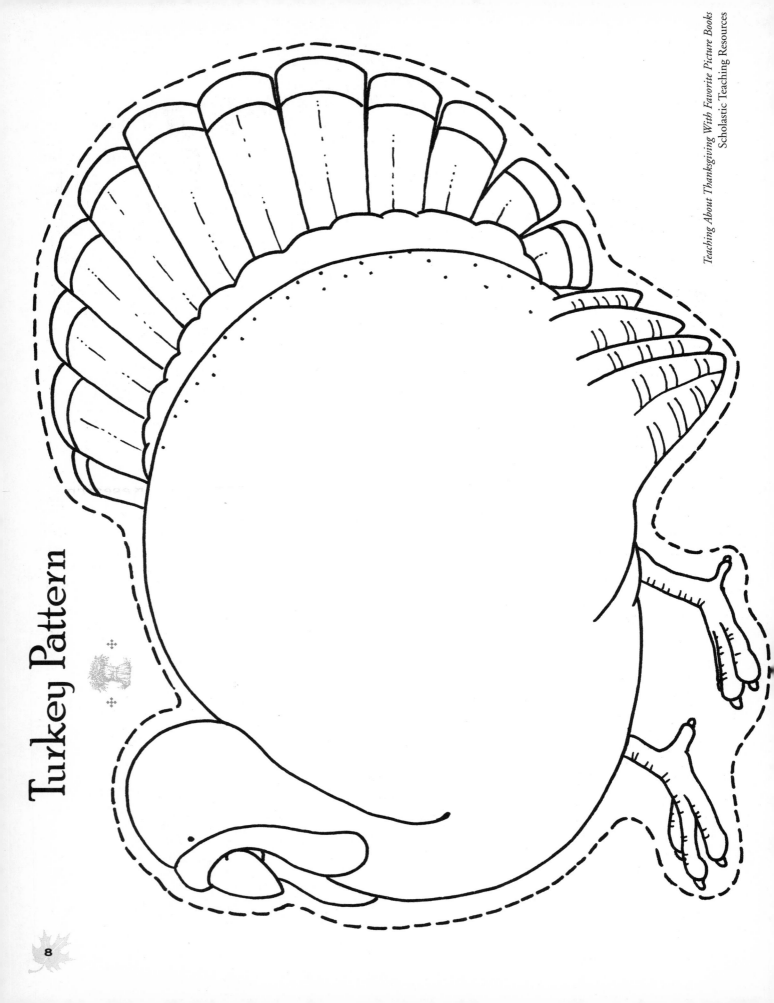

Turkey Pattern

Teaching About Thanksgiving With Favorite Picture Books
Scholastic Teaching Resources

On the Mayflower:
Voyage of the Ship's Apprentice
& a Passenger Girl

BY KATE WATERS
(SCHOLASTIC, 1996)

The voyage of the *Mayflower* to America is described through the experiences of William Small, the ship's apprentice. Excited, yet a little afraid, William begins the trip by performing routine duties. Then a storm comes, tossing the little ship to and fro, and William finds himself tying down equipment, repairing leaks, and caring for other crew members. All the while, he keeps a cautious watch over his new Pilgrim friend, Ellen, and the other passengers. With the storm finally behind them, the ship arrives in America, where William and Ellen strengthen their friendship as they await his departure back to England. Photos accurately portray the ship, events, and people in this reenactment of a historic journey.

The wild, stormy sea, as well as the cramped and unclean living conditions, caused the *Mayflower* travelers—especially the Pilgrims—much discomfort and illness. Ask children to share their thoughts on why both the crew and the Pilgrims were willing and determined to endure the hardships of their voyage. Then invite them to share their personal experiences about difficult trips they have taken.

Research Resources

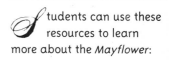

Students can use these resources to learn more about the *Mayflower*:

...*If You Sailed on the Mayflower* in 1620
by Ann McGovern
(Scholastic, 1991)

The First Thanksgiving: Voyage on the *Mayflower*

http://teacher.scholastic.com/ thanksgiving/mayflower

Caleb Johnson's MayflowerHistory.com

http://www.mayflowerhistory. com

Drama on the High Seas (Social Studies and Drama)

William and Ellen's journey across the Atlantic Ocean was truly a daring and dangerous adventure. Invite children to create personalized puppets to use in a reenactment of the story. First, have them color and cut out their choice of puppet patterns (page 14). To personalize their puppets, students can either draw their own features on the puppet face or cut out an opening for the face and back it with their photos. Then have children attach a wide craft stick handle to the back of their puppets. If desired, have them also color, cut out, and attach a handle to an enlarged copy of the *Mayflower* pattern (page 15). Display a length of blue bulletin board paper to serve as an ocean backdrop. Then invite students to act out the story in pairs or small groups, incorporating their puppets and creative "personal" experiences into the drama.

Westward Ho! (Social Studies)

The *Mayflower* set sail to travel west to America, but storms tossed it in all directions. Play this sailing game to help children learn the cardinal directions. To begin, have each child color and cut out the *Mayflower* pattern (page 15) and attach it to a fitted construction paper headband. Tape an X on the floor; then show children how to use a compass. To play, invite a child to don his or her headband, stand on the X, and take the compass (you might also display a large compass rose as an additional reference). Start by calling out a direction and distance (in footsteps)—for example, "North, three steps." Encourage the child to use the compass to find the given direction and "sail" the designated distance in that direction. Then call out another direction-distance combination, such as "East, four steps." Continue until the child's voyage ends at a classroom landmark, such as the math center, chalkboard, or teacher's desk. After each child has had a turn, ask students to set their headbands aside for use in "A Trip to Remember" (page 11).

Help children find England and North America on a large world map. Can they also find Cape Cod and Plymouth? In which state is Plymouth? Ask students to name the bordering states.

A Trip to Remember (Language Arts and Social Studies)

Give children each a copy of the poem on page 16. Then invite them to don their *Mayflower* headbands (from "Westward Ho!," page 10) and join in a choral reading of the poem. Afterward, have students cut out and mount their poems in the center of a large sheet of construction paper. Ask them to decorate the frame around the poem with related art. As an extension, give children a second copy of the poem and have them do the following:

◎ Write the syllable count to the left of each line.

◎ Underline pairs of rhyming words with same-color crayons.

◎ Circle the dates in the poem.

◎ Draw waves under the name of the ocean.

◎ Draw a face next to each verse to show the emotions of the travelers.

✶ A Class Compact ✶

*W*hile still on the *Mayflower*, the Pilgrims wrote the *Mayflower* Compact, a set of rules designed to help them live together peacefully and successfully. Have students draw up and sign a Class Compact. Display the document as a reminder of students' agreement to strive for a peaceful class community.

Mayflower Mobiles (Social Studies and Language Arts)

Until the voyage to America, the *Mayflower* had carried only cargo. But during its 1620 journey, the small ship was packed with 102 Pilgrims, their belongings, and about 30 crew members. After sharing this information with your class, have students research more facts about the *Mayflower*, its passengers, and the voyage to North America. Ask children to write their findings on a class chart. When completed, review the chart with students, then invite them to create these *Mayflower*-in-a-bottle mobiles.

1 Place a 4- by 7-inch transparency (or clear plastic page protector) over the *Mayflower* pattern on page 15. Use permanent markers or paint pens to trace the ship onto the transparency. Decorate the drawing with additional colors. (Allow the ink or paint to dry thoroughly before going to step 2.)

2 Cut scalloped waves along one long edge of a 3/4- by 7-inch strip of blue craft foam. Use rolled pieces of clear tape to attach the wave strip to the bottom of the *Mayflower* transparency.

3 Starting at the edge with the wave strip, roll the transparency into a tube shape. Insert the rolled transparency into a clear plastic 2-liter bottle (with label removed) and allow it to uncurl. Shift the bottle as needed to center the transparency so that the ship is upright.

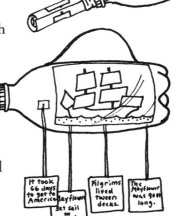

4 Use clear tape to attach a yarn hanger to the bottle. Cut several unlined notecards in half. Write a different *Mayflower* fact on each half. Using clear tape and yarn, attach each card to the bottle, as shown.

Tell children that space on the *Mayflower* was limited. Using the diagram in the book and other resources, have students draw and label the different compartments on an enlarged copy of the ship pattern (page 15). Ask them to explain how each area might have been used.

Meals on the ★ *Mayflower* ★

When the Pilgrims weren't too seasick to eat, they usually ate hard, dry biscuits and salted meat. To sample similar fare, serve children unsalted crackers and beef jerky. (Be sure to check for food allergies first.) Later, have students research and list other foods the Pilgrims ate on the voyage.

Packing for the Pilgrims (Language Arts and Reasoning)

Because the Pilgrims were moving to an undeveloped land, they had to pack a variety of materials for building and living. But the *Mayflower* was such a small ship that they also had to be selective in their packing. Display a large, simple cutout of the *Mayflower* and another of England. Explain the Pilgrims' packing dilemma to students; then divide the class into groups. Give each group a stack of sticky notes in a designated color. Then have children imagine themselves as Pilgrims moving to a new land. Show them a list of 20 items the Pilgrims might have considered packing for their trip. Have them write each item on a separate sticky note. Then tell the groups that they can take only 12 items from the list. Ask group members to decide together on which items to pack. Have them attach the sticky notes for these items to the ship cutout, and the remaining sticky notes to the cutout of England. When finished, ask each group to explain its packing decisions. To extend, repeat the activity with a list of different items.

fabric	weapons
seeds	fresh food
bed	jewelry
saw	shoes
pigs	money
wood	soap
tables	pans
spoons	chairs
pictures	books
glass windows	toys

Furl the Sails (Science)

When the storms began, the *Mayflower*'s crew furled, or wrapped, the sails. Ask children to give reasons for the crew's actions. Then invite students to experiment with a model sailing ship to learn how wind and sails work together. To make the ship, shape a piece of heavy-duty foil into a *Mayflower*-shaped boat. Tape a 2- by 2 1/2-inch paper sail to one end of a craft stick. Then press a lump of play dough into the bottom of the boat and plant the mast in it (figure 1). Have children place the ship in a water table or sink filled with water, blow air against the sail, and observe what happens. Next, have them remove the ship, roll the sail from bottom to top, and secure it with paper clips (figure 2). Then have students return the ship to the water and once again blow air toward the sail. Ask children to compare what happens now with their first observations.

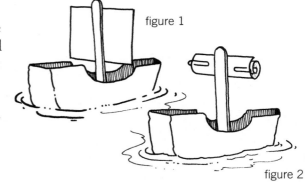

figure 1

figure 2

Math on the *Mayflower* (Math and Social Studies)

Have your young "math pilgrims" embark on an exciting journey into the world of math with these activities:

Related Reading

For an additional fact-based, fictional story about the Pilgrims' voyage, share with children **Across the Wide Dark Sea: The Mayflower Journey**, by Jean Van Leeuwen (Dial Books for Young Readers, 1995).

◎ Tell students that the *Mayflower* was about 90 feet long. In the gym or on a long sidewalk, have them measure and mark a distance of 90 feet with yarn. Then ask students to count and compare the number of paces it takes them to walk that distance. To extend, have children lie on their backs head-to-toe along the line. (If you have a small class, you might ask volunteers from another class to help.) Then ask them to count off to find out how many students fit on the line.

◎ The ceiling of the 'Tween Decks was five feet high. Label a two-column chart "Yes" and "No." Have children write their names on sticky notes and attach them to the chart to indicate whether or not they could stand upright under a five-foot ceiling. Afterward, measure each student's height and record it on his or her sticky note. Did students predict correctly? Later, have students sequence their sticky notes according to the height recorded on them.

Can I stand tall under a 5 foot ceiling?

YES		NO	
Marina 4ft. 1in.	Craig 4ft. 2in.	Mrs. Abeyta 5ft. 4in.	Ernie 5ft.
Joseph 4ft. 5in.			

◎ The *Mayflower* left England on September 6, 1620, and reached America on November 11. On its return trip, the ship left America on April 5, 1621, and arrived in England on May 6, 1621. Have children use a calendar to count the days from the beginning of the voyage to its arrival in America. Have them also count the number of days the *Mayflower* remained in harbor, and how long its return voyage to England lasted. To extend, ask students to convert all their totals to weeks, and the weeks to months. Have children explain how they arrived at their answers.

◎ The *Mayflower* weighed 180 tons! Ask children to add or multiply to find out how many two-ton cars are needed to match the weight of the *Mayflower*. Can they convert the ship's weight to pounds?

◎ After 66 days and 2,750 miles, the *Mayflower* finally reached America. Ask children to round the days to the nearest ten. Then have them use the rounded figure to compute the number of weeks the Pilgrims traveled. Finally, help them divide to find the estimated number of miles traveled in a week.

How many miles did the pilgrims travel each week?
70 days = how many weeks?
7 days in a week
$70 \div 7 = 10$ weeks
The pilgrims traveled for 10 weeks.
2750 miles ÷ 10 weeks =
275 miles/week
The pilgrims traveled 275 miles each week.

Drama on the High Seas Puppets

ship's apprentice

Pilgrim girl

ship's captain

Teaching About Thanksgiving With Favorite Picture Books
Scholastic Teaching Resources

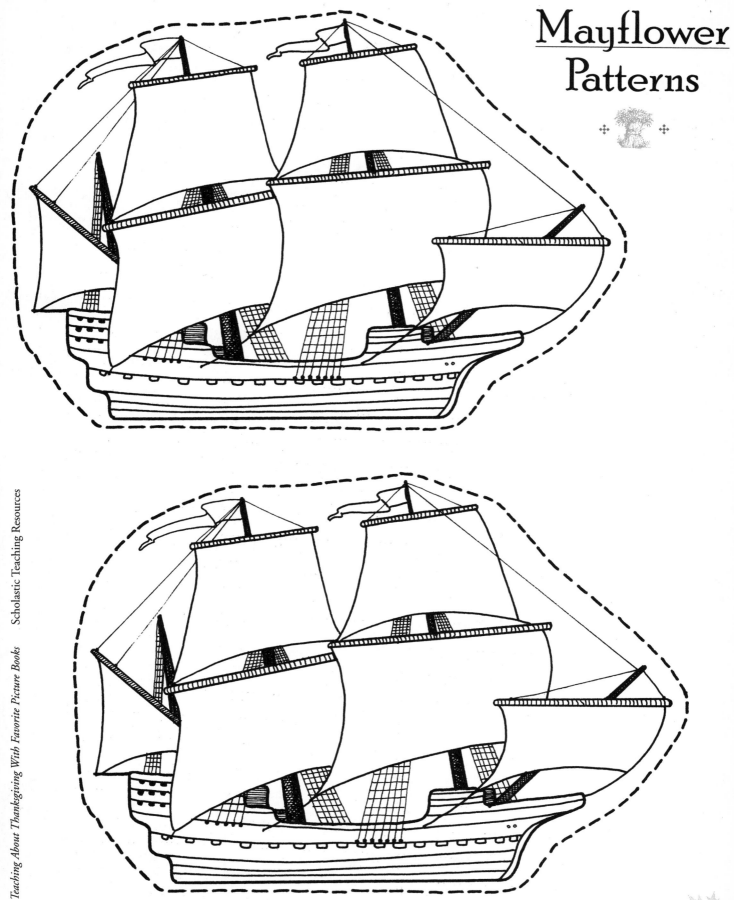

Mayflower
Patterns

A Trip to Remember

In 1620, the sixth of September,

A voyage began—a trip to remember.

102 Pilgrims and the *Mayflower* crew

Crossed the Atlantic waters of blue.

At the start, the weather was fair.

The ship sailed smoothly, without a care.

But then came a storm, and day after day,

Waves tossed the *Mayflower* every which way.

The skies finally cleared. The sea settled down.

Above, a voice called, "Land Ho! Dry ground!"

That November ninth, there arose a loud cheer,

"Hello, America! At long last we're here!"

by Immacula A. Rhodes

Teaching About Thanksgiving With Favorite Picture Books Scholastic Teaching Resources

The First Thanksgiving

BY JEAN CRAIGHEAD GEORGE
(PHILOMEL BOOKS, 1993)

panning the history of the Pilgrims' voyage and first year in America, this story highlights the experiences of Squanto (Tisquantum), and his relationship with the Englishmen. Squanto had been kidnapped by explorers and sold into slavery. After escaping to England, Squanto returns to his Pawtuxet village to find that his people have died of disease. He resides with a Wampanoag Indian community until he meets the Pilgrims, who are building new homes in his abandoned village. Familiarity, a desire to return "home," and his ability to act as an interpreter compel Squanto to stay with the Pilgrims. His lessons on fishing and farming as well as hunting and harvesting provide the colonists with essential survival skills that help them become healthy and productive in the new land. To celebrate their bounty and blessings, the Pilgrims plan a three-day feast of thanks, which Squanto and members of the Wampanoag people attend. (Note: In this book, the author states that the Pilgrims invited the Wampanoag to their feast. The actual circumstances under which Massasoit and 90 other Wampanoag attended are not known.)

Although cultural differences existed, the Pilgrims and Squanto developed a relationship. Discuss with children the history of Squanto's captivity and return to America. Ask them to share their thoughts on how Squanto may have felt about the English people. Why do they think he chose to be a helper instead of an enemy of the Pilgrims? (For more about Squanto's relationship with the Pilgrims and the Wampanoag, see page 24.)

Related Reading

Over the years, many myths have grown around the event known as the first Thanksgiving. In *Giving Thanks: the 1621 Harvest Feast* by Kate Waters (Scholastic, 2001), full color photographs record the reenactment of the first Thanksgiving at Plimoth Plantation (the living history museum that portrays life in seventeenth-century Plymouth, Massachusetts). The story and photos depict the events of the three-day celebration as historians think they really happened.

Extending the Book

Stepping Stones of History (Social Studies and Math)

When the Pilgrims stepped onto North American soil, they were stepping into history. Have children create this stepping stone timeline to show the historic events that occurred before and during Pilgrim times. To begin, cut out and label a large construction paper stone "Plymouth Rock." Display the stone—with a few sprouts of "grass" around its base. Then have children label additional smaller stone cutouts with events and dates mentioned in the book. Sequence and display the smaller stones to the right of the large one, creating a winding path of stepping stones. As students learn more about the events of Pilgrim times from other sources, invite them to add new stones to the display or fill in information on the existing ones. Use the display to reinforce students' math skills. For example, you might have children compute the number of days between two dates. Or ask children to find a specific event on the timeline and tell whether it happened before or after another event. Or have them find the corresponding date on the current year's calendar and tell which day of the week it falls on.

Plan a Village

Since Plymouth was to become their permanent home, the Pilgrims worked together to plan the village before building it. Have children work in small groups to plan and map out a small village. Ask each group to show and explain its plan to the class.

Pilgrim Houses (Social Studies and Art)

For homes, the Pilgrims built one-room frame houses with thatched (or grass) roofs. Have children make miniature Pilgrim houses from clean, individual-size milk cartons and various craft materials. Then invite them to use the houses to set up their own Pilgrim village.

1 Cut off the spout side of the milk carton.

2 Cut a slit in the raised ridge of the carton. Fold and glue the ridge down, as shown, to create a chimney. (Use a clothespin to hold the ridge in place while the glue dries.)

3 Cut out brown construction paper sides for the house. Fan-fold, then unfold, each piece before gluing it onto the carton. This will give the house a clapboard appearance.

4 Cover the chimney with brown paper.

5 Glue shredded strips of brown paper or raffia onto the roof.

6 Glue sand to the floor inside the house. Use additional craft materials to make interior furnishings to glue in the house.

To extend, children can also make milk carton *wetus* (WEE-to's), or Wampanoag houses, with these modifications:

◉ In step 2, do not cut the ridge. Instead, fold and glue the entire ridge down. After the glue dries, gently shape the roof and sides into a dome.

◉ Skip steps 3 and 4. In step 5, cover the entire house with shredded brown paper to represent bark.

Pilgrim Windows (Science)

The Pilgrims used oiled paper for windows instead of the glass panes used in England. Ask children to share their ideas about why the Pilgrims coated the paper windows with oil. Then invite children to use cotton balls to lightly coat manila paper with vegetable oil. Have them set their papers aside to allow the oil to soak in. Afterward, ask students to hold plain manila paper and the oiled papers side by side in front of a light and then over a colorful magazine page. Which paper allows more light and colors to show through? Next, have children sprinkle a few drops of water onto each paper and observe what happens. The water soaks into the plain paper but is repelled by the oiled paper. Explain that the Pilgrim's oiled-paper windows allowed some light into their dark homes and also helped keep rain out. To extend, invite children to draw Pilgrim scenes on manila paper, coat the papers with oil, and allow to dry. Encourage them to use their Pilgrim windows to explain to their families why Pilgrim homes had oiled-paper windows.

★ Research Resources ★

Let students get a close-up look at Pilgrim life in the 1600s. In **Easy Make & Learn Projects: The Pilgrims, the Mayflower & More** by Donald M. Silver and Patricia J. Wynne (Scholastic, 2001), students cut, fold, and tape to make realistic paper models of the *Mayflower*, the first Pilgrim town, a Wampanoag village, and more. Each lesson includes fascinating background information.

A Year of Seasons

In their first year in America, the Pilgrims experienced the four seasonal changes. Assign a different season to each of four student groups. Give each group bulletin board paper in a color related to their season and have them create a mural of the Pilgrims' activities during that season. Display the murals side by side in seasonal sequence.

An A-maize-ing Friend (Social Studies and Language Arts)

Just as the fish fertilizer boosted the growth of corn, or maize, Squanto's friendship helped the Pilgrims thrive during their first year in America. Discuss with children the qualities of friendship. Ask them to share ways in which Squanto was a friend to the Pilgrims. Then have students tell about ways in which they can be friends to others. To create a display on friendship, have children cut out the corn patterns (page 22), complete the sentence on each one, then color the cutouts. To assemble, help students staple the corn patterns together, as shown. Then display a large cutout of a basket. Attach the corn to and around the basket. Title the display "An A-maize-ing Friendship." Invite children to visit the display to read about Squanto's past acts of friendship and their classmates' current ones.

Colonial Food Pyramid (Science and Health)

Foods served during the first Thanksgiving differed from our present holiday dishes. Create with children a list of foods that were common during Pilgrim times. Then divide the class into groups and give each group a sheet of posterboard. Display a copy of the food pyramid. Then instruct groups to create a colonial food pyramid poster, filling in the section for each food category with names and pictures of Pilgrim foods. Afterward, invite each group to share its food pyramid with the class. To extend, have children fill in a food pyramid using present-day Thanksgiving foods.

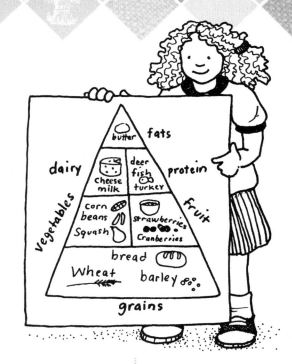

Thanksgiving Box Spinners (Social Studies)

To commemorate the Pilgrims' three-day Thanksgiving celebration, invite children to make these three-sided box spinners to help their families express holiday thanks.

1 To begin, children color the box pattern (page 23), glue it to tagboard, and then cut it out.

2 Next, they fold and glue the pattern to create a three-cornered box, as shown.

3 Then students use a paper fastener to attach the box to the bottom of a plastic bowl, making sure the box spins freely. (Help students punch a hole in the bowl using scissors.)

4 Finally, they cut a notch in the bowl, as shown.

5 To use, family members take turns spinning the box. They write on slips of paper things for which they are thankful that belong in the category that stops at the notch. Then they fold and place the papers in the box.

6 Encourage children and families to use the spinners daily (perhaps at each meal or at a family gathering). On Thanksgiving Day, families can read the paper slips one at a time and share their thanks for each thing named.

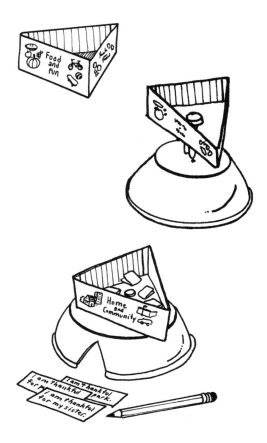

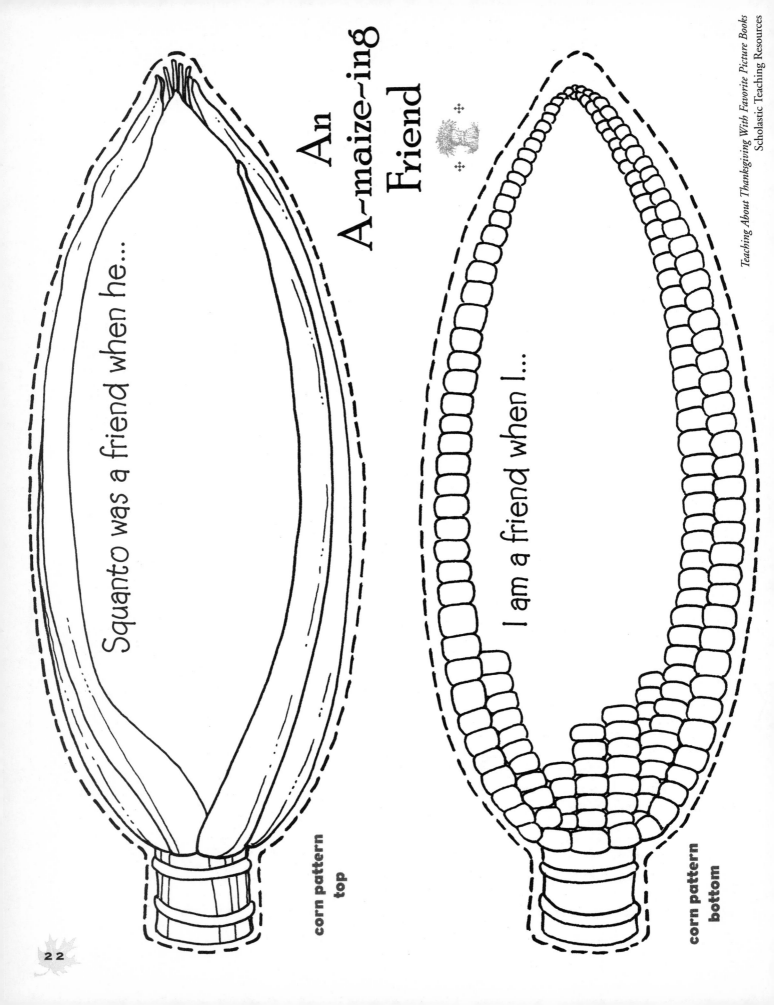

An
A-maize-ing
Friend

Squanto was a friend when he...

corn pattern top

I am a friend when I...

corn pattern bottom

Teaching About Thanksgiving With Favorite Picture Books
Scholastic Teaching Resources

Thanksgiving Box Spinner

Home and Community

Food and Fun

Family and Friends

Teaching About Thanksgiving With Favorite Picture Books
Scholastic Teaching Resources

23

Squanto's Journey:

The Story of the First Thanksgiving

BY JOSEPH BRUCHAC

(HARCOURT, 2000)

For another Wampanoag firsthand account, read Kate Water's *Tapenum's Day: A Wampanoag Boy in Pilgrim Times* (Scholastic, 1996). Then give students a close-up look at contemporary Wampanoag Indians carrying out old traditions by sharing *Clambake: A Wampanoag Tradition* by Russell M. Peters (Lerner Publishing Group, 1992), part of the *We Are Still Here: Native Americans* series.

In this first-person narrative, author Bruchac lets Squanto tell his own story—from befriending Captain John Smith to being captured and enslaved by the Englishmen to sharing in the first Thanksgiving celebration. He recounts how he came to live with the Pilgrims, teaching them the Wampanoag skills of hunting and fishing. And as he gives thanks for the bounteous harvest of their first year together, Squanto reiterates his hope that all who gather for this shared feast will share many more such days in the years that follow. (Note: Recently, based on information from primary source documents and Wampanoag oral tradition, an expanded view of Squanto has emerged. Some scholars today contend that he used his influential role in the Pilgrim and Wampanoag communities for his own ends.)

Trace with students the events of Squanto's life. On chart paper name each group of people that he lived with in his journeys; then discuss his experiences with each. Afterward, reread the last page of the book, emphasizing the phrase "all of our people." Ask children to share their ideas about what Squanto meant by these words.

Squanto's Scrapbook (Language Arts and Art)

Invite students to chronicle Squanto's many experiences in a class scrapbook. First, divide the class into two groups. Appoint one group to research Squanto's life before, during, and after captivity, up to the time he meets the Pilgrims. Have the other group research his life with the Pilgrims, including the first Thanksgiving. Instruct the groups to fill large sheets of construction paper with drawings and writings about Squanto's experiences. Encourage them to use their knowledge of the Wampanoag people, Pilgrims, lifestyles, and living conditions at that time. Children can use what they learn to imagine and write firsthand accounts of Squanto's interactions and dialogues with others, descriptions of his thoughts about a particular event, journal pages, and captions for their illustrations. Invite them to present their information in a variety of formats (poetry, narrative, collage, paintings, and so on). When finished, bind the pages between two construction paper covers and title the scrapbook.

★ What's ★ In a Name?

*W*ampanoag means "People of the First Light." Have children locate Massachusetts on a map. Explain that this is where the Wampanoag lived in Pilgrim times and continue to live today. Ask students to share their thoughts on why these people are so named. (For a clue, have them consider the sun's movement across the sky.)

The Three Sisters (Social Studies and Science)

Squanto showed the Pilgrims how to plant the "three sisters"—corn, squash, and beans—in mounds of soil, adding fish for fertilizer. The beans grew along the upright cornstalks and the squash spread along the ground to provide shade and choke out weeds. To help children understand how this plant trio grew, have them create these stand-up models of The Three Sisters.

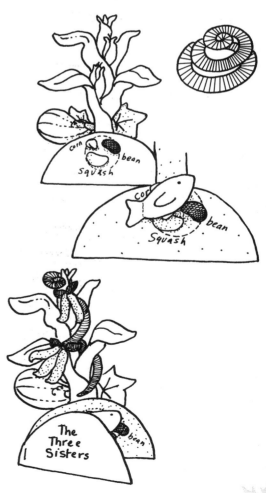

1 Color the patterns on page 28. Glue the corn plant and front flap to tagboard, then cut out all the shapes. Cut the bean vine in a spiral, as indicated.

2 Glue the squash plant to the back of the cornstalk.

3 Glue a real corn, bean, and squash seed to the dotted circle. Label each seed. Then dab glue only on the tail end of the fish, and place it over the seeds to create a flap.

4 Wrap the spiral bean vine around the cornstalk, as shown. Glue the string beans in place.

5 Staple the front flap to the corn plant on the left side.

6 To display, slightly open the front flap and stand the model on a flat surface.

The Wampanoag have an attitude of thanksgiving every day. They hold Thanksgiving celebrations for other special occasions, such as a child's birth, the honoring of ancestors, seasonal harvests throughout the year, and other gifts from the earth. On paper corn, bean, and squash shapes, have children write things for which they give daily thanks. Place the shapes in a basket, then read a few aloud whenever you have extra moments to fill.

Trials and Triumphs (Social Studies and Character Education)

In his lifetime, Squanto experienced a number of trials and triumphs. Explain these terms to students, then create a two-column chart, using each word as a heading. Invite children to list each of Squanto's experiences on the chart under the most appropriate heading. After reviewing the chart, tell children that everyone experiences both trials and triumphs. Ask them to quietly think about their own challenges and victories since the beginning of the school year. Then have children create similar charts listing their personal trials and triumphs. Collect the charts, then take time later to chat with each child about his or her chart. Be sure to praise the child's triumphs and provide encouragement for the trials. If possible, help the child brainstorm solutions to overcome his or her trials.

Squanto's Trials	Squanto's Triumphs
captured and made a slave	returned to his home
learned that his people died of disease	learned to live with new group of people
taught Pilgrims how to survive	enjoyed the harvest with Pilgrims

3-D Wampanoag Models (Social Studies and Art)

Explain that the Wampanoag of the seventeenth century used all-natural resources for their clothing. Then have children examine their attire in the book. List each article of clothing along with the natural material that was possibly used to make it. Afterward, invite small groups to create three-dimensional models of Wampanoag people. First, assign a common craft item to represent each material used by the Wampanoag—for example, brown butcher paper can be used for animal skin, yarn for hemp laces, craft foam for shell beads, and craft feathers for feathers. Then have each group trace the outline of a child on bulletin board paper. Have groups cut out the body tracings and use the assigned craft materials to create Wampanoag clothing for their cutouts. Have them use additional craft materials for the face and other details of their models. For ideas and accuracy, encourage students to refer to the pictures in the book as well as other resources (see Related Reading, page 24 and Research Resources, page 27). Have children add notecards describing each article of clothing on their completed models. Then display the projects for all to enjoy.

turkey feather
shell necklace
pouch
hemp belt
breechclout
Mantle
pouch for corn
leggings
elkskin moccasins
shells

Pouch for a Pniese (Language Arts, Character Education, and Art)

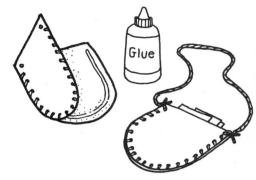

While hunting or traveling, the Wampanoag of the seventeenth century carried pouches filled with *noohkik*, a parched corn that was used for nourishment. But each Wampanoag who had the title of *pniese* (pa-NEES)—a counselor and warrior—also had to nourish his character with the traits that earned him this title: honor, courage, wisdom, and kindness. Invite children to make pouches that hold reminders of the special qualities of a pniese. To make the pouch, children color and cut out the pouch and card patterns (page 29), adding designs to the cutouts as desired. Then they glue the pouch together where indicated. When the glue dries, students punch a hole in each side of their pouches and tie on a yarn hanger. They write one trait of a pniese on each card and insert the cards in their pouches. While children wear their pouches, periodically ask them to remove a card, read it, and tell about a way in which they exemplify that quality. (As a variation, children may use the pouch pattern as a template for making felt pouches. They can decorate their pouches with paint pens and then sew them with a large needle and yarn.)

Wampum Jewelry (Social Studies, Character Education, and Art)

★ Research Resources ★

For information on the Wampanoag people, visit **www.plimoth.org** or **www.bostonkids.org/ teachers/TC**.

Or read *People of the Breaking Day*, by Marcia Sewall (Atheneum, 1990).

The Wampanoag, among other Native peoples of the seventeenth century used small purple and white quahog clamshell beads, known as wampum, as symbols of power and authority. Use wampum in this small group activity to help children identify character traits that give them power and authority in their own lives. First, dye rigatoni to use as large wampum. Simply fill a shallow pan half-full with water. Then stir in purple or white washable paint until the liquid takes on a deep coloring. Dip the rigatoni, then set it on waxed paper to dry.

For the activity, write different character traits on 1- by 4-inch slips of paper. Wrap each tightly around a pencil, slip it off, and insert it in a piece of wampum. Place the wampum beads in a basket. To use, children take turns choosing a bead, removing the paper (using the end of a pencil), and reading the character trait. Each child tells whether he or she possesses the named trait and, if so, shares a way in which it is displayed.

To follow up, children can make wampum character necklaces. To do this, they color and cut out the shell medallion (page 29). Then they fold and staple the cutout to a length of yarn, as shown, leaving the medallion free to open and close. On the inside of the medallion, they write character traits that describe themselves. Finally, children string dyed rigatoni wampum (and beads, if desired) on either side of the medallion, tie the yarn ends together, and hang the necklace around their necks.

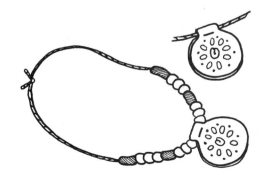

The Three Sisters

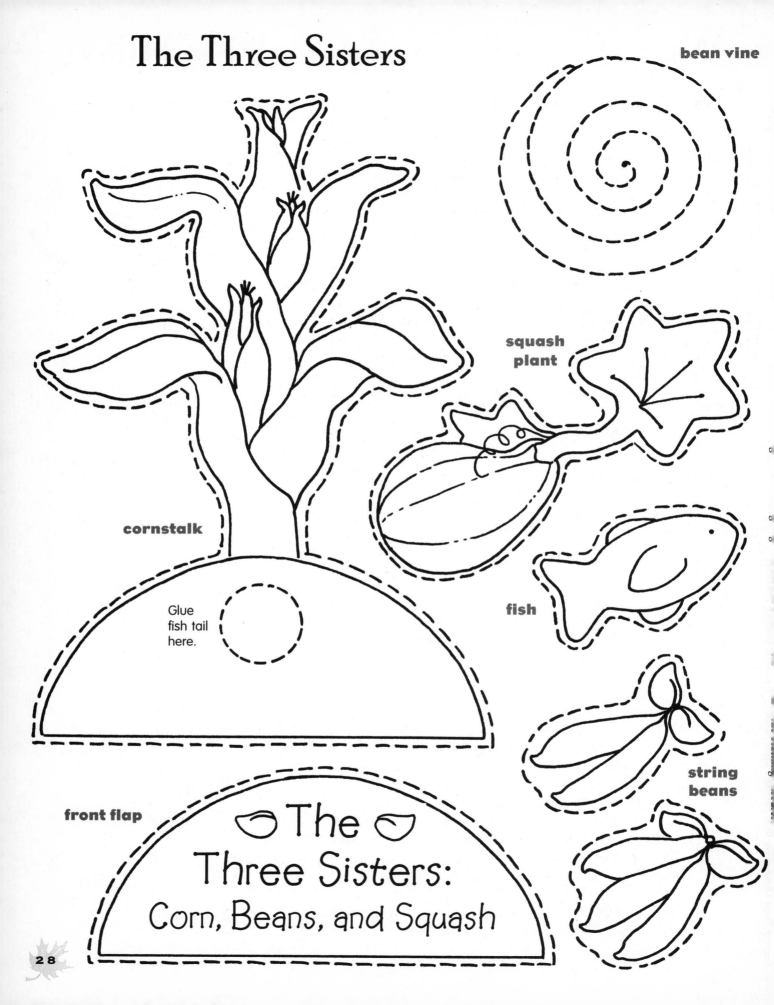

bean vine

squash plant

cornstalk

Glue fish tail here.

fish

front flap

The
Three Sisters:
Corn, Beans, and Squash

string beans

28

Wampanoag Pouch and Shell Medallion

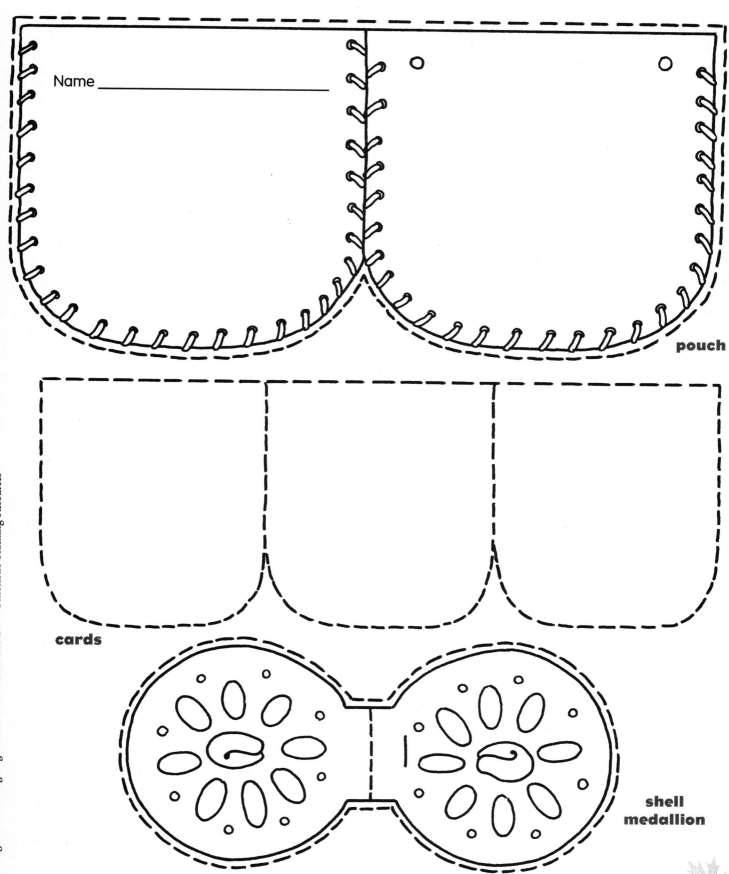

Name _____

pouch

cards

shell
medallion

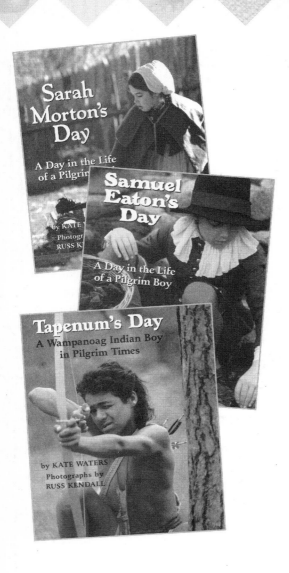

Sarah Morton's Day:
A Day in the Life of a Pilgrim Girl

BY KATE WATERS (SCHOLASTIC, 1989)

Samuel Eaton's Day:
A Day in the Life of a Pilgrim Boy

BY KATE WATERS (SCHOLASTIC, 1993)

Tapenum's Day:
A Wampanoag Indian Boy in Pilgrim Times

BY KATE WATERS (SCHOLASTIC, 1996)

In this trilogy about life during Pilgrim times, each book explores the daily activities of a different child. Readers journey with the child from sunrise to sunset, gaining insight into the nature of his or her chores, experiences, thoughts, and feelings. Amidst daily routines, each child takes a little time to dream and plan for the future. Sarah Morton wants to be able to read letters to her mother; Samuel Eaton hopes to help with the harvest; and Tapenum, a Wampanoag youth, sets in action his training plan to become a *pniese*, or warrior counselor. Photographed at the living history museum at Plimoth Plantation in Plymouth, Massachusetts, these books portray the people of colonial days and their living and working conditions in an accurate, interesting, and educational format.

Discussion Starters

The children in these stories all had responsibilities and chores to do. Write each of their names on chart paper, then ask children to list the jobs for each child. Afterward, discuss the work each child performed and how he or she contributed to the community. What responsibilities do children have today, and how do they contribute to our society or community?

All in a Day's Work (Social Studies and Language Arts)

A Pilgrim's day was ruled by chores and responsibilities. To understand how busy young Pilgrims were, have students create a story-strip timeline to show the daily schedule of a made-up Pilgrim child. First, have children cut several 9- by 12-inch sheets of white construction paper in half lengthwise. Then help them glue the strips together end to end to make one long strip. Instruct children to accordion-fold their strips into 4-inch-wide sections and then title the first section "_____'s Day." Next, ask them to describe and illustrate each remaining section with one of the child's daily activities. When finished, have students compare the timelines for each Pilgrim. To contrast a Pilgrim's day with one of their own, children might also create a timeline to show their activities.

Newspaper for a New Land (Social Studies and Language Arts)

Invite children to create a class newspaper about Pilgrim times. To begin, pair up children to work together as reporters. Have each pair research a book character or real person who lived during Pilgrim times. Then have students write and illustrate an article about their chosen Pilgrim. For additional newspaper features, ask each pair to create an ad, weather report, article on planting and crop conditions, or other related piece. Encourage children to write each piece to reflect the language and culture of the times. To make the newspaper, have students label a strip of paper "The Pilgrim Times" and then cut out and glue the strip over the banner of an actual newspaper. Ask them to glue their articles and other pieces directly onto the newspaper as well.

Chore Charades

Have each child in a small group act out a chore from one of the books. Challenge the group to identify the chore as well as the character performing it.

Related Reading

Read with your class **The Pilgrims of Plimoth**, by Marcia Sewall (Atheneum, 1986), or **Three Young Pilgrims** by Cheryl Harness (Bradbury Press, 1992), to learn more about Pilgrim life.

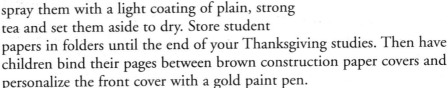

Experience Journals (Language Arts)

Create quill "pens" by attaching feathers to a
few pencils. Put the quills in your writing
center, along with plain paper. Have children
use the materials to write personal accounts of
their imaginary experiences as Pilgrims or
native people (they might also include
experiences prior to the Pilgrims' arrival in
America). To age their papers, students can
spray them with a light coating of plain, strong
tea and set them aside to dry. Store student
papers in folders until the end of your Thanksgiving studies. Then have
children bind their pages between brown construction paper covers and
personalize the front cover with a gold paint pen.

Aim for the Goal (Social Studies)

Sarah, Samuel, and Tapenum each had individual goals for themselves.
Help students state their goals with this *petan* (pee-TAN), or quiver, filled
with arrows.

1 First, ask children to fringe three 4- by 10-inch sheets of brown
construction paper.

2 Have them glue the fringed
paper in layers around a tall
potato chip canister so that it
resembles a quiver covered with
animal fur.

3 To make a strap, help children
tape one end of a length of yarn
to the inside top of the quiver and
the other end under the middle row
of fringe.

4 For arrows, ask children to
cut out and decorate several
12-inch posterboard arrows.

5 Have them write a goal (or a
way to achieve one of their
goals) on each arrow and insert it in
the petan. Later, invite children to
share their petans, and goals, with
the class.

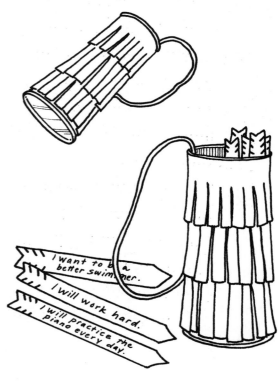

✹ Practice ✹
Patience

*T*apenum understood
that he needed to be
patient about learning new
things. Discuss with students
some skills and activities
which require patience to
learn well. Invite each child
to write one such skill on a
class list.

Colonial Clothes Closet (Social Studies)

Pilgrim children wore clothes very different from today's styles. Invite children to play this modified Go Fish game to learn about the clothing of Pilgrim times. To prepare, copy, color, and cut out two sets of matching clothes cards (page 34). Then cut out the game boards on page 35. Laminate the cards and game boards.

◎ To play, each child in a pair selects a game board and takes eight cards from the deck. The remaining cards are placed facedown on the table.

◎ Players check their cards for matching pairs of clothes that also match a square on their game boards. If a match exists, they place the cards on the game board. (Because the stockings and shoes Pilgrim boys and girls wore were very similar, players may use these cards interchangeably to fill in their Pilgrim Boy and Girl game boards.)

◎ Then player 1 names a card in his or her hand. If player 2 is holding a corresponding card, he or she gives it to player 1.

◎ If not, player 2 says "Clothes Closet" and player 1 draws a card from the deck. If a match can be made with the new card, player 1 places it on the game board. Play then proceeds to player 2.

◎ The game continues in this manner until a player has covered all the pictures on his or her game board.

Colorful Clothes

Popular images show Pilgrims dressed in only black and white, but their clothing was actually very colorful. They often wore garments that were bright blue, red, green, and yellow. Invite children to color their choice of enlarged Pilgrim clothes cards (page 34). Then have them cut out the pictures on the cards and glue them onto self-portraits to create images of themselves dressed as Pilgrims.

Buckles and Beads

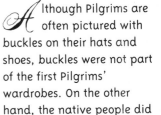

Although Pilgrims are often pictured with buckles on their hats and shoes, buckles were not part of the first Pilgrims' wardrobes. On the other hand, the native people did wear beads. Invite children to create beaded necklaces using yarn, beads, and other materials such as pasta tubes and cut straws.

Colonial Clothes Closet

clothes cards

Pilgrim Boy

breeches	doublet	points
hat	stockings	shoes

Pilgrim Girl

petticoat	waistcoat	apron
coif	stockings	shoes

Oh, What a Thanksgiving!

BY STEVEN KROLL
(SCHOLASTIC, 1988)

For additional reading, share *The Pilgrims and Me*, by Judy Donnelly (Grosset & Dunlap, 2002), *Fat Chance Thanksgiving*, by Patricia Lakin (Albert Whitman & Company, 2001), and *Thanksgiving Day*, by Gail Gibbons (Holiday House, 1983).

Read to your class *Thank You, Sarah: The Woman Who Saved Thanksgiving*, by Laurie Halse Anderson (Simon & Schuster, 2002), to learn how Sarah Hale worked for years to make Thanksgiving a national holiday. (See page 41 for more about this book.)

Convinced that his family celebration is not as exciting as the real Thanksgiving, David lets his imagination carry him back in time to Plymouth Colony and the first Thanksgiving. He imagines voyaging to America on the *Mayflower*, living in a thatch-roofed house, hunting turkey, and dressing like a Pilgrim. While lost in his imaginings, David meets his teacher, who helps him see—just in time—that his modern Thanksgiving is as real and exciting as the Pilgrims' first celebration.

Ask children to share ways in which their Thanksgiving celebrations are similar to or different from the Pilgrims' first celebration. Like David, do they ever wish they could experience life during Pilgrim times? Invite groups of students to act out Thanksgiving Day, first from the Pilgrims' perspective, then from their personal experiences.

Past and Present Venn Diagram

(Social Studies, Math, and Logical Reasoning)

Compare past and present Thanksgiving activities with a Venn diagram labeled "Thanksgiving Today," "Thanksgiving Then," and "Both," as shown. Have children name activities, events, foods, and so on, that are related to Thanksgiving. Decide together whether their responses are related specifically to the first Thanksgiving, to today's holiday, or to both. Then ask students to record their responses in the appropriate space on the diagram. When finished, review and discuss the diagram.

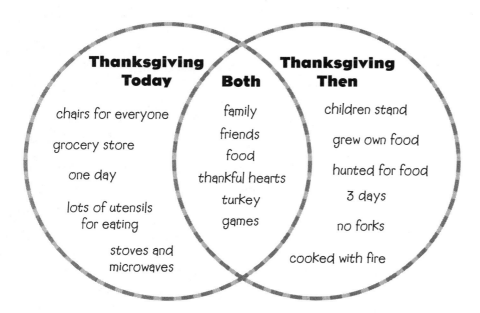

Thanksgiving Today

chairs for everyone

grocery store

one day

lots of utensils for eating

stoves and microwaves

Both

family
friends
food
thankful hearts
turkey
games

Thanksgiving Then

children stand

grew own food

hunted for food

3 days

no forks

cooked with fire

Community Maps (Social Studies)

In the story, David and Mr. Sanderson surveyed their neighborhood from a hill. Ask children to draw and label maps of their neighborhoods. Then have them affix a smiley sticker to each place on the map for which they are thankful. Encourage children to share their maps with a classmate, then later with their families.

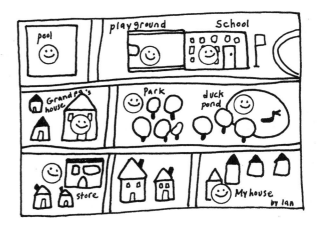

★ **Thoughts** ★
of the Future

*A*sk children to draw cartoon frames of Pilgrims engaged in different activities, adding thought bubbles to show them imagining future ways they might perform their activities. For example, a field worker might imagine riding a tractor, or a cook using a microwave oven.

Pilgrims in the Present (Social Studies, Drama, and Language Arts)

David thought it would be fun to live in Pilgrim times. Invite children to imagine they meet a Pilgrim in present times. How will they explain present-day routines and devices such as the telephone, television, cars, planes, and microwave ovens? After they have thought through some explanations in their minds, group children in pairs. Have each pair create a Pilgrim body poster by drawing a life-size clothed Pilgrim's body—from the neck to knees—on a sheet of posterboard (students might trace a child's body in pencil to use as a guide). Then invite one child, wearing a Pilgrim hat or coif (see page 64 for easy-to-make versions), to hold the poster in front of him- or herself and take the role of a Pilgrim. Have the other child "walk" the Pilgrim through a day in the present. Encourage the Pilgrim to ask questions about things that he or she would not have had experience with in Pilgrim times. Afterward, have partners switch roles. Finally, ask children to write about and illustrate things they learned, as Pilgrims, about the modern world. If desired, bind their pages into a class book titled "Pilgrims in the Present."

Combined Culture Thanksgiving Stories (Language Arts)

Invite children to use these story wheels to combine past and present traditions and cultures to create Thanksgiving stories. First, have children color and cut out the wheel patterns on pages 39–40. Then have them stack the wheels by size, with the largest on the bottom. Help them attach the wheels to a paper plate with a paper fastener and then cut two notches in the plate rim, with the notches opposite each other, as shown. To use, children align a picture on each wheel with a notch. Then they make up imaginary Thanksgiving tales—realistic or fantastic—involving the designated people, places, and things on the wheels.

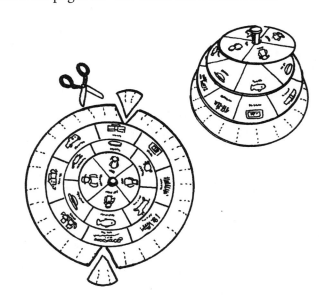

people wheel

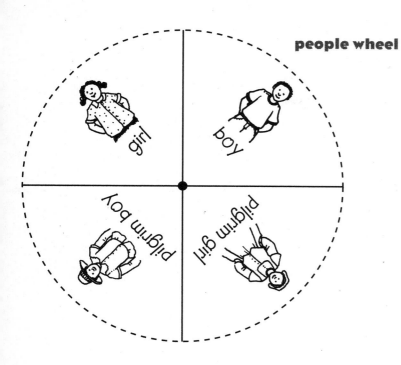

Story Wheel

objects wheel

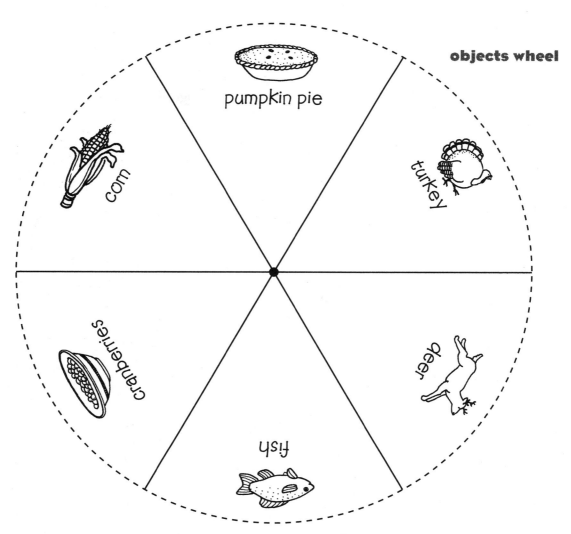

Story Wheel

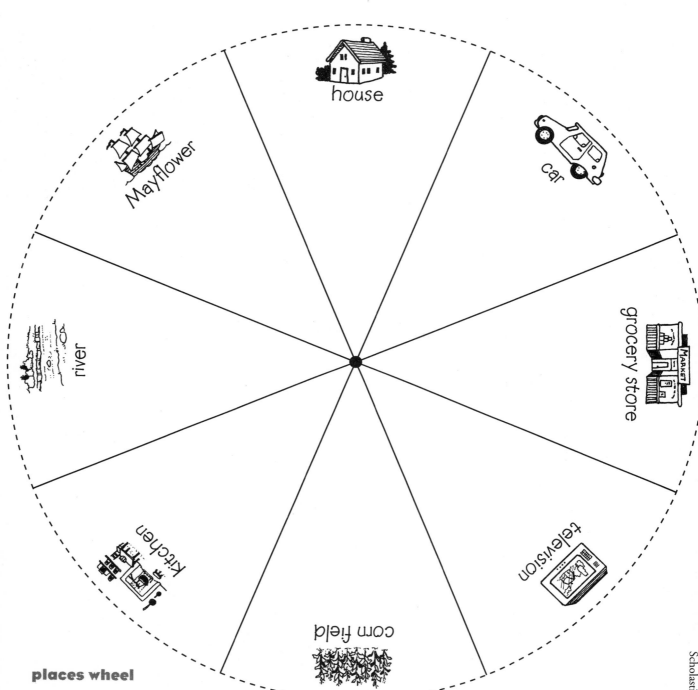

house

car

grocery store

television

corn field

kitchen

river

Mayflower

places wheel

Teaching About Thanksgiving With Favorite Picture Books
Scholastic Teaching Resources

Thank You, Sarah:
The Woman Who Saved Thanksgiving

BY LAURIE HALSE ANDERSON
(SIMON & SCHUSTER, 2002)

Looking beyond traditional Thanksgiving stories, this book pays tribute to Sarah Hale, who crusaded tirelessly to make Thanksgiving a national holiday. As an editor and author, Sarah penned numerous letters about her cause to readers, politicians, and presidents. After 38 years, five presidents, and thousands of letters, Sarah finally succeeded when Abraham Lincoln agreed that the United States needed a Thanksgiving holiday to bring the country together. Humorous, colorful characterizations punctuate historical figures and events in this delightful, true tale about a bold, brave, stubborn, and smart lady who saved Thanksgiving for us all.

Discuss Sarah Hale's persistence and how she must have felt when she finally accomplished her goal. Invite children to tell about their experiences in being persistent and the results. Did they achieve what they set out to do? To extend, encourage children to keep a record of their stick-to-itiveness. First, ask children to write a goal on a large blank notecard. Post each child's card in his or her personal space in the classroom. For each day that the child "sticks" to doing what is necessary to achieve the goal, have him or her draw a simple self-portrait on a small sticky note and affix it to the card. When a child achieves a goal, announce the accomplishment to the class and reward the child with a small token. After a designated time, reward the persistence and accomplishments of all students by having a class celebration.

Feather-Pen Timelines ✯

*I*nvite children to cut out construction paper feather pens and label each with one of Sarah's efforts to make Thanksgiving a national holiday. Have them sequence and glue the cutouts end to end, then take the feather-pen timelines home to share with their families.

Special Thanks ✯

*H*ave children write thank-you cards or notes to Sarah Hale. Ask them to include why they are thankful that she saved Thanksgiving. Then pretend to be Sarah and read each child's card or note. Verbally respond to students as you think Sarah might have done.

Thanksgiving Hero Tubes (Language Arts, Social Studies, and Art)

In this book, Sarah Hale is a superhero because she saved Thanksgiving. Who are your students' Thanksgiving heroes? Figures from the past, such as Squanto, Edward Winslow, Abraham Lincoln, or Sarah Hale? Or someone in the present, such as a parent, relative, friend, or teacher? What makes these people heroes to students? To commemorate their Thanksgiving heroes, invite children to create hero tubes. To begin, have children decorate a paper towel tube with glitter crayons or pens. Then ask them to complete page 44, roll up their hero pages, and insert them in the decorated tubes. Have them close one end of the tube with a square of tissue paper and rubber band. Then invite children to add a handful of confetti and crinkle-cut paper strips to the tube and close the other end with another tissue paper square and rubber band. Encourage children to open and share their hero tubes during their family Thanksgiving celebrations.

Mighty Pens (Language Arts and Character Education)

When children write these letters of praise to classmates, they'll discover firsthand how mighty the pen can be—and how much joy it can bring. First, label slips of paper with students' names and place them in a paper bag. Have children draw names from the bag, keeping their selections a secret. Afterward, ask children to write anonymous letters of praise to their selected classmates. Have them fold the letters, seal them in envelopes, and write the recipients' names on the front. Collect all the envelopes in a mailbag. Later, draw one letter at a time from the bag and pass it to the child named on the envelope. Let the child read the letter silently, then aloud if he or she chooses. Then watch joyous smiles spread as readers and writers alike share the positive power of printed praise.

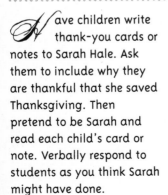

Turkey Talk (Language Arts and Art)

Review with children the pages in the book that show pictures of turkeys. How do these birds feel about all the talk of Thanksgiving? After discussing, have students draw a two-frame cartoon by dividing a sheet of drawing paper in half. Ask them to illustrate the first frame with a turkey from long ago, before Thanksgiving became a national holiday. Then have them draw a speech bubble and label it with something the turkey might say about the idea of a Thanksgiving holiday (this can be humorous or serious). Have children illustrate the second frame with another turkey, including a speech bubble that shows a statement about today's Thanksgiving holiday. Invite children to share their cartoons with the class.

Persuasive Pencils (Language Arts)

Set up a writing center to promote persuasive writing. To begin, cut out a large quill pen and inkwell from bulletin board paper. Label the quill cutout with "Writing Works," then display the cutouts in your writing center. Explain to students that even today we can write leaders about ways to better our school, community, state, or country. Ask them to share ideas about ways to make their school a better place—perhaps more playground equipment, a schoolwide announcement board, or a different routine for lunch. Or maybe they have ideas for improving a particular classroom routine. List students' responses on a chart. Then have them visit the writing center to write letters persuading school leaders to make the proposed changes. Encourage children to include reasons for making the changes as well as the improvements they will bring about. Have students read their letters to the class or, if desired, deliver them to the appropriate school leaders.

No Thanksgiving, ★ No...What? ★

*B*rainstorm with students all the things that we would have to do without if there were no Thanksgiving—such as parades, large family gatherings, turkey leftovers, and a holiday from school and work. Ask children to tell about the things they would miss most.

Presidential ★ Power ★

*L*ist the presidents that Sarah Hale wrote letters to. Have children research each one to discover when he became president, how long he served, and major events and decisions that occurred during his term.

_____'s Thanksgiving Hero

Here is a picture of my Thanksgiving hero.

The name of my Thanksgiving hero is

_____.

This person is my Thanksgiving hero because

_____

_____.

Here are more reasons why I admire my Thanksgiving hero.

_____

_____

_____

Teaching About Thanksgiving With Favorite Picture Books   Scholastic Teaching Resources

It's Thanksgiving

BY JACK PRELUTSKY

(HARPERCOLLINS, 1982)

From the very first Thanksgiving to the leftovers from last year's celebration, this collection of poems covers the anticipation, excitement, and challenges of our nation's favorite holiday. Clever rhymes, coupled with entertaining illustrations, express the heart of Thanksgiving experiences across the land, leaving readers amused and inspired.

After reading the poems to your class, ask children to tell which poems were most meaningful to them and why. Then invite children to combine their imagination, creativity, and Thanksgiving knowledge and experiences to write and design poems to display in class. Some students might write their poems in stacked verse while others arrange their text into the shape of a turkey or pumpkin, or wrap the verses around an illustration. Some children might write their poems on seasonal shapes while others surround their verses with colorful borders. After children complete their poems, have them display their work on a laminated sheet of bulletin board paper titled "Thanksgiving Poetry Panel."

Related Reading

Share additional Thanksgiving poems with students, from *Thanksgiving Day at Our House*, by Nancy White Carlstrom (Simon & Schuster Books for Young Readers, 1999). Other books written in rhyme include *Round the Turkey*, by Leslie Kimmelman (Albert Whitman Co., 2002), and *Today Is Thanksgiving!*, by P. K. Hallinan (Ideals Children's Books, 2001).

After we eat on
Thanksgiving Day
The grownups
always get sleepy.
But even when the
sky is gray
My uncle takes my
cousins and me
Out to the park
to play!

★ "If Turkeys ★ Thought"

After sharing this poem from the book, invite children to color and cut out the turkey pattern on page 8 and glue it to construction paper. Then have them write turkey escape thoughts on speech bubble cutouts (for example, "I'm going to pack my bags and catch the next plane out of here!"). Ask children to glue the speech bubbles to their turkey pictures.

Personal Thanksgiving Scrolls (Language Arts)

After reading the poem "It's Happy Thanksgiving," discuss with children ways in which Grandma makes her grandchild happy on Thanksgiving. Then invite students to create scrolls for those who make their Thanksgiving a happy day. First, have them write and illustrate a verse about the special person on a sheet of paper. The verse might include what they do with the special person on Thanksgiving or why they give thanks for that person. Then have them roll up and tie their scrolls with ribbon. Finally, encourage each child to present his or her special person with the scroll on Thanksgiving Day.

Special November Quilts (Social Studies and Art)

Use the poem "The Middle of November" to prompt a brainstorming session about things children associate with the month of November. Student responses might include past and present Thanksgiving-related activities as well as things related to the weather, season, or local events for the month. After listing their responses on chart paper, give children 6-inch squares of paper to decorate with November-related pictures. Then piece the completed squares together to create a class quilt display titled "November Is Special!" Invite children to point out and tell the class about their quilt squares in the display.

Wishes on Dishes (Language Arts)

Read "The Wishbone"; then ask children to share their experiences with wishing on wishbones. Afterward, invite them to make these wishbone booklets to share with their families. First, have students color and cut out several copies of the wishbone booklet page (page 48). Ask them to write about and draw a Thanksgiving wish on the back of each page. To make a front cover, have children color and cut out only the wishbone from a copy of the booklet page. Ask them to glue the wishbone to a 9-inch paper plate and title the cover "My Thanksgiving Wishes." Finally, have students stack and staple their pages between the front cover and another paper plate.

Class Parade Viewer (Social Studies and Art)

After reading "The Thanksgiving Day Parade," discuss students' experiences with watching and participating in parades. Then invite them to make a class parade viewer.

1 Have children draw and label their parade favorites on 8 1/2- by 11-inch sheets of white paper, positioned lengthwise.

2 Tape the drawings together end to end to create a parade strip, adding a blank page to each end of the strip.

3 To make a parade viewer, cut a 10- by 8-inch opening out of the front of a tall, hinged-lid laundry detergent box with a handle. Also cut a 9-inch vertical slit on each side of the box.

4 Close and glue the lid to the box. Then glue silver foil wrapping paper to the box, leaving the opening and slits uncovered and the handle exposed.

5 Once completed, thread one end of the parade strip through the side slits of the viewer so that the pictures can be seen from the front opening.

6 Tape each end of the strip to separate paper towel tubes and roll the strip around one tube as far as possible. To use, two children work together to scroll the parade strip through the viewer while classmates watch the parade go by. Invite children to narrate the parade and provide music and sound effects to give it a realistic feel.

Related Reading

Read ***Milly and the Macy's Parade***, by Shana Corey (Scholastic, 2002), to launch a discussion about the multicultural influences that shaped the 1924 Christmas parade in New York, now known as the annual Macy's Thanksgiving Day Parade.

Wishes on Dishes

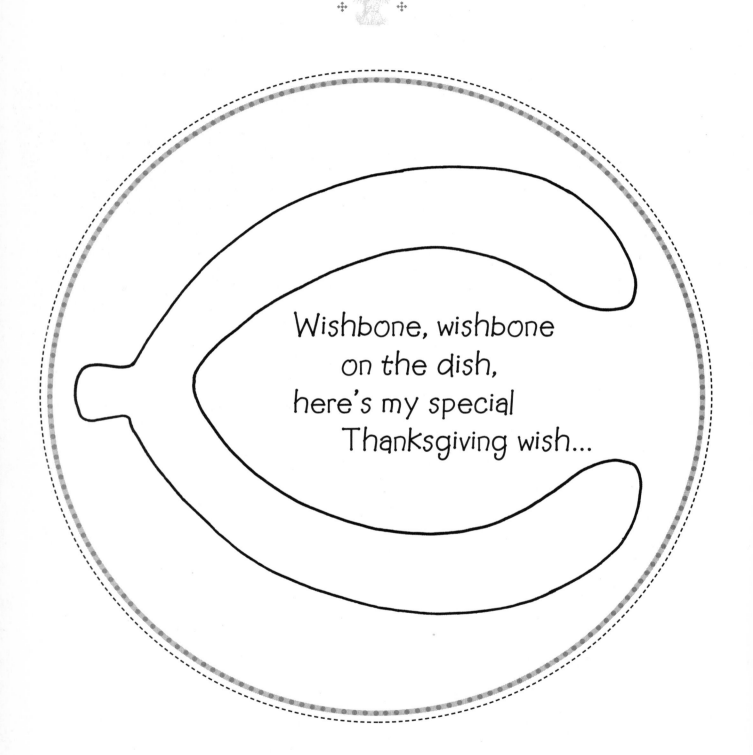

Wishbone, wishbone
on the dish,
here's my special
Thanksgiving wish...

Teaching About Thanksgiving With Favorite Picture Book
Scholastic Teaching Resource

48

'Twas the Night Before Thanksgiving

BY DAV PILKEY
(ORCHARD BOOKS, 1990)

A class trip to Farmer Mack Nugget's turkey farm turns into tears and chaos when the schoolchildren discover what lies ahead for their new feathered friends. Taking action in their time of crisis, the children come up with a clever rescue plan that leads to a Thanksgiving filled with love and happiness for everyone—except the baffled Mack Nugget.

Reread the first four pages of the book. Ask students to recall words and phrases that describe the kind of day on which the story takes place. What season is it? Explain that the author used descriptors to help establish the mood and setting of the story. Brainstorm with children a list of words and phrases that describe sights, smells, and sounds of the fall season. Then invite students to create rhymes about an imaginative ride on an autumn day, using words from the list. If possible, have them set their verses to the meter of a familiar rhyme. Invite children to recite their rhymes to the class, adding actions and sound effects if they desire.

Additional stories about hatchet-escaping turkeys include:

◆ *Gracias, the Thanksgiving Turkey* by Joy Cowley (Scholastic, 1996)

◆ *A Turkey for Thanksgiving* by Eve Bunting (Clarion House, 1991)

◆ *One Tough Turkey: A Thanksgiving Story* by Steven Kroll (Holiday House, 1982)

◆ *Sometimes It's Turkey— Sometimes It's Feathers* by Lorna Balian (Abingdon Press, 1973)

Extending the Book

Turkey Rescue! (Math)

Invite students to play this basic facts game to rescue turkeys from the chopping block. Have children color and cut out the game board and the numbered turkey cards on pages 52–53. Then have them select eight cards to place on the turkey pen. To play, call out one addition fact at a time. If children have the answer on a turkey card, they rescue that turkey from the pen by moving it to the bus. The first child to rescue all of his or her turkeys wins the round. To reinforce basic subtraction, multiplication, or division facts, simply write answers to the desired facts on the blank cards (page 53). Then have children cut out and use these cards in the game. (NOTE: When not in use, children can store their game cards in zippered sandwich bags.)

Who Took the Turkey? (Logical Reasoning and Language Arts)

Children use clues to discover the turkey thief in this modified version of Who Took the Cookie From the Cookie Jar? To prepare, copy the turkey pen and eight blank turkey cards (pages 52–53), enlarging them if desired. Then color, cut them out, and laminate. Seat children in a circle, placing the turkey pen full of turkeys in the center. To play, a child takes the role of farmer and leaves the room. Another child removes a turkey from the pen and hides it on him- or herself. (For variety, more than one child might take a turkey.) The farmer returns, checks the pen for missing turkeys, then asks,

"Who took a turkey from the turkey pen? Did _____ take a turkey from the turkey pen?" The farmer fills a child's name in the blank. If the named child does not have the turkey, he or she responds, "Not me!" The farmer answers, "Then who?" The child then says, "Someone with _____ took the turkey from the turkey pen," filling in the blank with a feature of the turkey thief, such as hair color or shoe description. Play continues in this way until the turkey thief is identified. The turkey thief takes the role of the farmer for the next round of play.

Gobble, Gobble, Giggle (Science and Language Arts)

Children will get the straight facts on turkeys with this fun game. First, ask them to color and cut out the two-sided puppet pattern on page 54. (Have them set the fact cards aside for later use.) Then have them fold the puppet in half and glue it to a craft stick, as shown. To use, read a fact card to students, leaving out the word in parentheses. If the statement is true, children show the turkey side of their puppets and say "Gobble." If false, they turn their puppets to the child side and give a giggle. To test their knowledge further, you can include additional true and false turkey statements. Afterward, have children cut out their turkey fact cards. Then invite them to take their cards and puppets home to play with family and friends.

Related Reading

Read **A Thanksgiving Turkey**, by Julian Scheer (Holiday House, 2001), to learn interesting facts about turkey behavior.

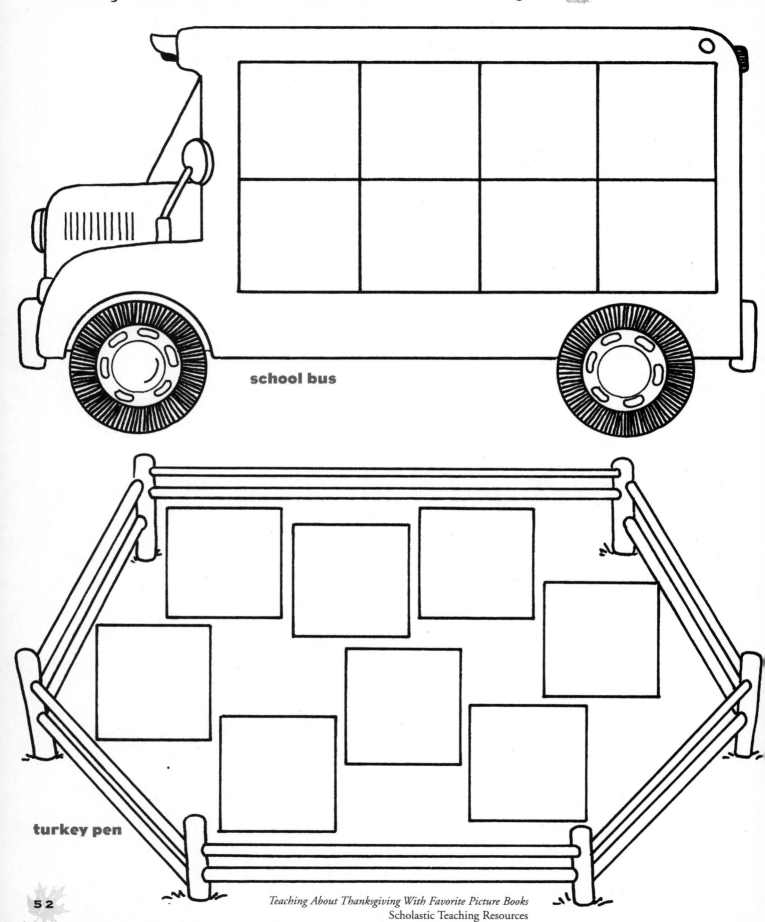

school bus

turkey pen

Turkey Rescue! *and* Who Took the Turkey? ❖🦃❖ **turkey cards**

Teaching About Thanksgiving With Favorite Picture Books   Scholastic Teaching Resources

Gobble, Gobble, Giggle

turkey fact cards

Turkeys can run up to 25 miles per hour. (Gobble)	"Gobble" is the only sound made by turkeys. (Giggle)
A male turkey is called a tom. (Gobble)	All turkeys have beards. (Giggle)
The brown feathers of a turkey hen help camouflage the bird. (Gobble)	Turkey eggs are the smallest bird eggs. (Giggle)
Turkeys see well in the daytime, but not at night. (Gobble)	A turkey uses its wattle to store extra food. (Giggle)
The piece of skin above a turkey's beak is called a snood. (Gobble)	A turkey's head and neck are covered with feathers. (Giggle)
The male turkey fans its colorful feathers to attract a mate. (Gobble)	Turkeys eat only three meals a day. (Giggle)

puppet pattern

Teaching About Thanksgiving With Favorite Picture Books   Scholastic Teaching Resources

A Plump and Perky Turkey

BY TERESA BATEMAN
(WINSLOW PRESS, 2001)

With Thanksgiving approaching and no turkeys in sight, the citizens of Squawk Valley devise a plan to lure a bird to town. Using an art show as a ploy, the townsfolk capture the attention of a turkey named Pete, who arrives to model for the local artists. As honorary guest, Pete is also asked to stay and judge the art show. While the crowd hungrily cheers the special guest, clever Pete makes a camouflaged escape, taking along an oatmeal souvenir and leaving Squawk Valley with wall-to-wall turkey—but not one plump and perky—for its Thanksgiving feast.

The people of Squawk Valley created posters advertising the position for a turkey model. Did their method get results? Ask children to brainstorm other ways the citizens might have lured a turkey to their town. Afterward, invite students to create "Wanted" posters for a turkey to fill the position of friend or helper for themselves.

Research Resource

*A*lthough considered silly and unintelligent, turkeys are actually very clever birds. For the smart facts on turkeys, visit the National Wild Turkey Federation Web site at **www.nwtf.org/all_about_turkeys/wild_turkey_facts.html**.

Turkey Snack Mix

*E*xplain that Pete took the oatmeal art because turkeys eat plant foods similar to oatmeal—seeds, berries, acorns, nuts, and so on. Then have children create a turkey mix by combining a variety of snack foods representing different parts of a turkey's diet. After enjoying their snacks, students can write a turkey-mix recipe to share with their families. (SAFETY NOTE: Check for food allergies before serving snacks to children.)

Extending the Book

Word-Family Balloons (Language Arts)

Turkey families of different sizes ballooned out of Squawk Valley as Thanksgiving approached. Invite children to create word families of different sizes with these balloons and turkeys. First, ask them to color and cut out the patterns on page 57, cutting the slit in the balloon where indicated. Then have them write a word-family ending on the balloon. Next, instruct children to write on each turkey a letter that can be used with the word-family ending to create a word. (They can use as many cutouts as they wish.) Ask them to insert their turkeys in the slit in the balloon. Finally, have students write each new word on the balloon basket. Or have them write a sentence using words from the word family.

Turkey Sculptures (Art and Logical Reasoning)

Creating turkey art seemed so simple to Ebenezer Beezer. Was the task easy for the actual artists? Provide children with a variety of substances that can be shaped by hand, such as soapsuds, shaving cream, stiff oatmeal, mashed potatoes, and cream of wheat. Then challenge them to create turkey art from the substance of their choice. If desired, have available extra materials that students might use for the internal structure of their sculptures—for example, pipe cleaners, toothpicks, and craft sticks. For fun, take photos of the sculptors and their creations to display in class.

Camouflage Collage (Art and Visual Skills)

Pete disappeared into the collage of turkey art, where he was camouflaged, or hidden, from the townspeople's sight. Invite children to create a turkey collage using the turkey pattern on page 8. To use the cutout as a template, have children outline the turkey on decorative wrapping paper or wallpaper samples and then cut out the shapes. Or have them use markers to create patterns and designs directly on the cutout. When completed, display the turkeys in a collage. Then invite children to use the display in a game of I Spy a Turkey. To play, one child at a time describes a particular turkey in the collage for classmates to identify.

Word-Family Balloons

This Is the Turkey

BY ABBY LEVINE

(ALBERT WHITMAN & COMPANY, 2000)

In this holiday tale, set to the rhythm of "The House That Jack Built," Max's anticipation builds as he helps choose and cook the Thanksgiving turkey. His excitement rises as family and friends arrive with their dinner contributions. At long last, the turkey's done and it's dinnertime! With spirited enthusiasm, Max leads his mother to the table, but fails to see the toy on the floor in front of him. The resulting accident causes the turkey to fly off the plate and sends poor Max into tears of grief and frustration. The understanding words and expressions of love from his guests help Max overcome his disappointment, and he goes on to enjoy his best Thanksgiving yet.

Related Reading

These books also emphasize the importance of togetherness at Thanksgiving:

◆ *Thanksgiving at the Tappleton's* by Eileen Spinelli (HarperCollins, 1984)

◆ *Turkey Pox* by Laurie Halse Anderson (Albert Whitman & Company, 1996)

◆ *Daisy's Crazy Thanksgiving* by Margerie Cuyler (Henry Holt and Company, 1990)

Happy Gatherings (Social Studies)

Thanksgiving Day is a time to gather with family and friends. Page through the book with children to review the guests at Max's Thanksgiving gathering. Then invite children to think about their own family gatherings. Ask them to illustrate large sheets of construction paper with their favorite Thanksgiving activities that include all guests. Have them label each person in their drawings. Then give students notecards cut in half. Ask them to write something interesting about each person on a separate notecard and then glue each card near the drawing of that person. Encourage children to share their drawings at their family Thanksgiving gatherings.

Holiday Highs and Lows (Social Studies and Handling Emotions)

High ☺

Doreen helped cook the turkey.
Keisha made a touchdown.
Marty got the last piece of pie.
Danielle danced for the family.

Low ☹

Doreen fell in the mud.
Keisha got a toothache.
Marty missed the parade.
Danielle ripped her favorite skirt.

With the turkey roasting and guests arriving, the holiday was in full swing and Max was feeling high with excitement! Then the accident happened. How did Max feel after the accident? How did he overcome his disappointment? After the discussion, invite children to share their Thanksgiving highs and lows with this activity. To prepare, divide a sheet of chart paper horizontally into two wide rows. Draw a large smiley face and write "High" next to the top row. Then draw a sad face and write "Low" next to the bottom row. Ask one child at a time to tell about a personal Thanksgiving high and low. Did he or she overcome the low feeling? How? At the end of each child's turn, write a brief sentence to describe the child's experiences in the corresponding rows on the chart.

Gracias, the Thanksgiving Turkey

BY JOY COWLEY (SCHOLASTIC, 1996)

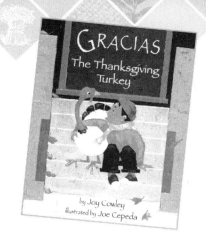

When Miguel reaches the train station to pick up a present from his truck-driver father, he's surprised to find a turkey in a crate. Tasked with fattening the turkey for Thanksgiving, Miguel names the bird Gracias and the two become fast friends. As Miguel learns to care for Gracias, his family, friends, and neighbors all pitch in. And they all sympathize with him when the turkey is stolen from her outdoor cage. Fortunately, Gracias is returned, only to follow Miguel to church, where an unexpected blessing helps save her from becoming the family's Thanksgiving meal. Vivid oil paintings and Spanish text sprinkled throughout add to the pleasure of this story.

Gracias, Amigos (Language Arts)

Encourage children to express their thanks for classmates, teachers, volunteers, and school helpers with this paper bag turkey. Invite children to finish the sentence "I am thankful for…" with a name and why they are thankful for that person. Have them fold and deposit their papers in the turkey bag. Then, whenever you have extra time, pull out a few papers and read them. Later, encourage children to give their papers to the people named on them.

1 Fold down the top of a large paper bag and fringe it as shown.

2 Color the turkey head (page 60), glue it to tagboard, cut it out, and add a large wiggle eye. For the neck, cut out a slightly curved 2- by 10-inch strip of cardboard. Glue the head to the neck.

3 Use the turkey leg (page 60) as a template to cut out two orange construction paper legs.

4 Cut several sheets of colored construction paper in half lengthwise. Cut feather shapes from these.

5 Write "Gracias, Amigos" on a large index card. Glue the sign to a wide craft stick.

6 Attach all the pieces to the fringed paper bag, as shown.

Gracias Means Thank You

Give children copies of the turkey on page 8 to color and cut out. Have them add thanksgiving sentences using the word *gracias*. For example, a child may write "Gracias, Mom, for making my favorite turkey burritos for Thanksgiving!" Invite children to give their turkeys to the people to whom they are expressing thanks.

Pet Turkey Tales (Language Arts and Social Studies)

Write Spanish words from the story and the English meanings on chart paper. Also add other Thanksgiving- and family-related Spanish words that students would like to learn (use a Spanish-English dictionary as a reference). Then have children write a story about an imaginary pet turkey, using Spanish words from the chart whenever appropriate. Later, invite children to read their stories to the class. Each time a Spanish word is used, have the class give its English translation.

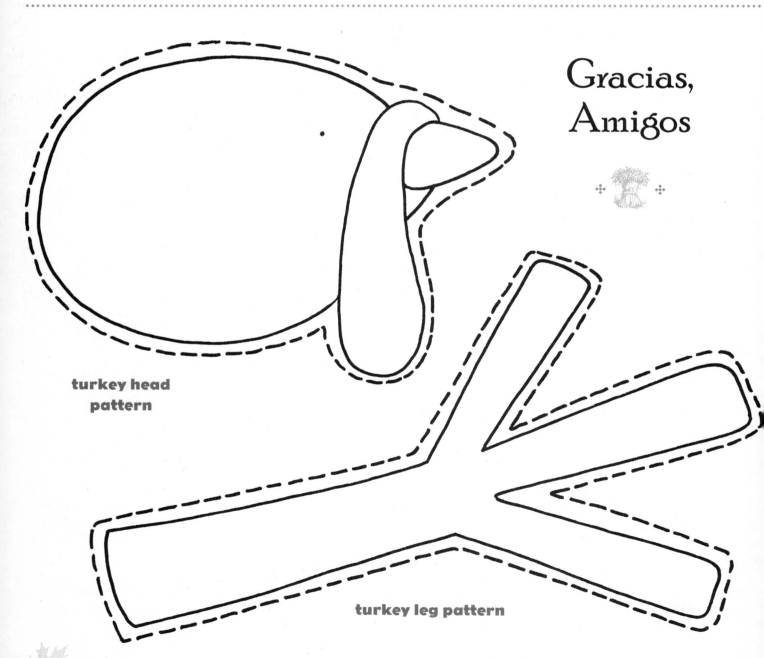

Gracias,
Amigos

turkey head
pattern

turkey leg pattern

Rivka's First Thanksgiving

BY ELSA OKON RAEL
(MARGARET K. MCELDERRY BOOKS, 2001)

Rivka, the child of Jewish immigrants new to America, is learning all about Thanksgiving at school. But when she asks her family if they can celebrate the holiday, Bubbeh turns the decision over to Rabbi Yoshe Preminger. At first, the Rabbi is not convinced that Thanksgiving is a day for Jews to celebrate. But in a bold and determined move, Rivka explains that Thanksgiving is for all Americans, and she persuades the Rabbi to rethink his decision. The result? A traditional Thanksgiving celebration blended with traditions from Rivka's own Jewish culture.

Reasons to Give Thanks (Social Studies and Language Arts)

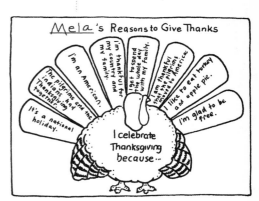

The blend of traditional Thanksgiving foods with Jewish dishes was a way in which Rivka's family expressed their thanks for America and its traditions as well as their own cultural traditions. Invite children to tell about and express appreciation for unique traditions or foods related to their family celebrations. Then explain that, just as Rivka said, Thanksgiving is for all Americans. Each of us celebrates the holiday for many reasons. Have children fill in the turkey feathers (page 62) with reasons for which they celebrate Thanksgiving. Then invite them to color their pictures. Afterward, have each child share his or her turkey with the class.

An Invitation to Celebrate (Social Studies and Language Arts)

Rivka's grandparents were a few of many who immigrated to America in the early 1900s. Often, these newcomers didn't know about the history and traditions of the Thanksgiving holiday celebrated in the United States. This is true for many immigrants even today. Have children create cards that give (or show) a simple explanation of Thanksgiving as celebrated in the U.S. Ask them to fold sheets of construction paper in half. On the inside, have children include an invitation for the imaginary newcomer to join them for the holiday. Display the cards with the title "Thanksgiving Is for Everyone."

Related Reading

To read more multicultural Thanksgiving stories, share *Molly's Pilgrim*, by Barbara Cohen (Lothrop, Lee & Shephard, 1983), and *Thanksgiving Wish*, by Michael J. Rosen (Blue Sky Press, 1999).

_____'s Reasons to Give Thanks

I celebrate Thanksgiving because...

Teaching About Thanksgiving With Favorite Picture Books
Scholastic Teaching Resources

A Class Thanksgiving Celebration

Use these ideas to host a Thanksgiving celebration sprinkled with foods, customs, and games from Pilgrim times. While setting up for your celebration, display students' favorite holiday books and projects for guests to enjoy.

Add some authenticity to your celebration with these ideas:

- Ask parents and caregivers to bring in foods or dishes eaten during Pilgrim times. You might send home a food list that includes nuts, pumpkin seeds, dried cranberries, currants or raisins, along with some recipes, from which they can make their selections. (See resources, right.) Ask families to let you know in advance which foods they will be contributing to the class feast. Then check for food allergies before serving the foods and dishes to students and guests.

- Invite children to wear head coverings that represent the fashion of Pilgrim times. (See Pilgrim Coifs and Hats, page 64.)

- Encourage children to serve their parents and guests. Ask each child to stand beside his or her parent (or guest) at the table during the meal, as Pilgrim children did.

- At the beginning of the meal, distribute plastic knives and spoons to guests. Explain that these were the only utensils used by Pilgrims. (Later in the meal, you might pass out forks on request.)

- Give each student and guest a strip of three to four attached paper towels. Have them drape their large napkins over one shoulder to use for wiping their fingers and mouths, as the Pilgrims did when they dined.

Continued on next page.

Research Resources

Eating the Plates by Lucille Recht Penner (Macmillan, 1991). This wonderful book offers a wealth of information about the food preparation, cooking techniques, and home life of the Pilgrims. The book also includes a section of authentic Pilgrim recipes such as Fresh Corn Soup, Red Pickled Eggs, and Bannock Cakes.

The Thanksgiving Primer (Plimoth Plantation Publications, 1991). This comprehensive guide includes fascinating background information and recipes, such as Stewed Pompion (Pumpkin) and Furmenty (a sweet and spicy boiled wheat pudding), to help you recreate the first harvest festival.

Colonial Fun and Games

In advance, prepare the following games. After your class feast, invite students and guests to participate in a few of these modified colonial games:

- ◎ **Knickers:** Cut out notches from the edge of a shoe box. To use, players turn the box over and try to shoot marbles into the box through the notches. The player with the most marbles in the box wins.

- ◎ **Pin Game:** Punch a hole near the rim of a small plastic cup. Tie one end of a string to the cup. Tape the other end to the end of an unsharpened pencil. To use, players take turns catching the cup on the end of the pencil.

- ◎ **Pitch the Bar:** Cut a foam swimming noodle in half to use as a bar. Players take turns throwing the bar as far as possible.

- ◎ **Stool Ball:** Place a stool (or overturned box) in the center of a circle. Have players stand around the circle. Invite one player at a time to use his or her forearm to "bat" a beachball toward the stool target. The player with the most hits on the target wins the game.

Pilgrim Coifs and Hats

Pilgrim girls and women often wore tight-fitting linen bonnets, called *coifs*. Men and boys usually wore felt hats.

1. To make a coif, copy and enlarge the pattern, opposite. Then cut it out.
2. Fold a sheet of white legal-size (8 1/2 by 14 inches) paper in half, the short way.
3. Trace the pattern onto the folded paper, as shown. Then cut it out.
4. Tape as shown.
5. Clip to the head with bobby pins.

1. To make a pilgrim hat, copy and enlarge the pattern, opposite, onto brown, tan, or black construction paper, using the measurements shown. Then cut it out.
2. Have children cut a 1-inch hatband out of construction paper (any color), about 7 inches long, and glue it to the hat.
3. Measure and cut out a paper headband, about 2 by 24 inches, for each child.
4. Have children glue the part of the brim directly below the hatband to the headband. (The ends of the brim should not be glued down.)
5. Fit the headbands to children's heads and staple or tape closed.